C000065200

RICHARD PRICE was born in 1966 ... d
at Napier College, Edinburgh an... 1
th... 1
Sc... ...ce
his ... 1993, including *Lucky Day* (Carcanet ...), which was a
Gu... ...ook of the Year and shortlisted for the Whitbread Poetry Prize.
In ... his poem 'Hedge Sparrows' was chosen to represent Team GB in
the Olympics project 'The Written World'. His poems have been widely
anthologised, and translated into French, Finnish, German, Hungarian and
Portuguese. He is also a short story writer and novelist, a critic, and the
editor of the little magazine *Painted, spoken*. He is Head of Content and
Research Strategy at the British Library, in London. Richard Price's
website is at www.hydrohotel.net.

Also by Richard Price from Carcanet Press

Lucky Day
Greenfields
Rays

RICHARD PRICE

Small World

CARCANET

First published in Great Britain in 2012 by
Carcanet Press Limited
Alliance House
Cross Street
Manchester M2 7AQ

www.carcanet.co.uk

Copyright © Richard Price 2012
The right of Richard Price to be identified as the author of this work
has been asserted by him in accordance with the
Copyright, Designs and Patents Act of 1988

A CIP catalogue record for this book is available from the British Library
ISBN 978 1 84777 158 2

The publisher acknowledges financial assistance from Arts Council England

Supported by
ARTS COUNCIL
ENGLAND

Typeset by XL Publishing Services, Tiverton
Printed and bound in England by SRP Ltd, Exeter

for the patient, and for the Patient

My name is Double Double This This,
Double Double That That,
Double This, Double That,
Double Double This That

England, Ireland,
Scotland, Wales –
Inside, Outside,
donkeys' tails!

stand on the elastic

I have a best friend:
she's a chocolate biscuit.

Acknowledgements

The epigraph contains fragments from playground songs first published in *Painted, spoken* and transcribed from performances by Ellen Price and Maisie Price. 'Faster!', arranged by the author, is taken from a song sung by Ellen Price in the same survey. 'An old drawer up beyond the children' first appeared in Julie Johnstone's one poem project, *less*.

Other poems collected here were originally published in *Alba Londres*, *Cahiers intempestifs*, *cul de qui*, *The Lyre*, *Magma*, *Manhattan Review*, *Poetry Review* and *The Red Wheelbarrow*.

'Jazz syllabus' appeared in *An Unofficial Roy Fisher* (Shearsman) and 'I am greatly changed' within *A Mutual Friend: Poems for Charles Dickens* (Two Rivers), both edited by Peter Robinson.

An alternative version of 'House martins' was first published in *Birdbook 1* (Sidekick), edited by Jon Stone and Kirsten Irving; 'Delicate greenery' and 'Pinnacle wordfinder' were first published by *likestarlings*.

Both 'Blue black permanent' poems appeared in the letterpress collection *Frosted, melted* (diehard), and 'Left neglect' in *Adventures in Form* (Penned in the Margins), edited by Tom Chivers.

Versions of many of the poems collected here were recorded in a single session for the online Archive of the Now, curated by Dr Andrea Brady, Queen Mary, University of London.

My thanks to all involved, and to Judith W., Peter McC., Sandy H., and David K.

"In memory" is dedicated to the late Fiona Farquhar.

Contents

SMALL WORLD

AFTERWORD

SMALL WORLD

An old drawer up beyond the children

Little torn-offs, kept, gummed, and a bill window; large small change in matt grey and bronze. 'Are these your medals, Dad?'

A list of do-it-ourselves in feet and inches. Half-hollow plastic letters, red red, blue blue. They won't, can't, endure an open word. Grr – consonant consensus.

A single staple, not yet folded, in self-assembly dust.

Up beyond the children this old drawer, laden (can stick). Easy with it, extract and show.

A double-planet system –
the Earth and the Moon.

Stability,
maybe stability.

And maybe the moon – you know –
an equal – once.

Sisters – (a little big-sister,
a big little-sister) –

rough couplets,
two haloes of pressure,

mutual, unequal –
the solidarity of interference.

(Their desire to hold.
Their desire to hold back.)

Cocktail hour

Measure out, administer.

Katie's half dribbling, half tiny-bubbling.
She's laughing (gentle). She's not swallowing this, tells it
in a viscous mumble, bright red –
to Miss Piggy on her night-top.

A lip froth of light pink. Epilim
is the trademark; the mixer saliva.

Cheers.

Cheers.

<

Measure out, administer.

A balancing spoonful – red's liquid thisness accepted
but a no-swallow repeat. The jaws grip.

A slow worrying; the spoon's dog-stickish.
I'm pulling carefully this side, carefully that.
Katie is *teeth*. (By the way,
either animals are not animals or we are all animals.)
Her head moves with me:
she seems to know and she seems to No. Eye contact, smiling. Finally
we are free. The spoon looks wiped clean (tight lipped Katie). No,

no swallow. She's
snorting an avoidance –
turning, turning with a backward shove. The drug-thick syrup still not down.
Now she's… this way, facing close with a face-full. Her cheeks are puffed up,
pursing, pursing, (drama of the mime), twice tight-lipped. She pouts,
full of it.
She twitch-teases. She

blurts.

<

We have both dyed. *That's sis-gusting!* (– big little-sister Ellen, suddenly
                                                                        at my side).

We're all a crimson speckling (our faces, my peevish glasses).
We are red-spectrum endpapers, delicate, an art house horror clip.
We are blood relations.

Measure out.

Administer.

Tuning out and seeking scrap,
any marker to don't-know down a page.

Tuning out.
We'll not be bullied by gangsters in Ellen's gel pen.
We'll not be bullied by gangsters on a white sheet
of printer fodder – surrender all news
to glitter strawberry
and the scent of glitter strawberry scent.

A6ing the A4.

I'm just full of the Cuban infant mortality rate.
How come you don't like your own kids in America?

Casting the first statistic,

                              a little folded

<

/and over the fold
seeking cutting adage
no, simpler, an artist's book itinerary

slow up

(a keyboard waits six years
for EDCD EEE- DDD- EEE-
EDCD EEE- DDED C—)

wherever she would go
wherever she would go

<

The house asleep I'm a Special Effect, a digital ghost,
not quite random with the poked remote:
boxed-in music and the truth channelled uncanny by current affairs.

'Rhythm is a dancer' – Katie was a drummer.
The djembe's decoration now
and she's all eyes for the boy bands.
There's Newsnight unanimity, Late Night Revue
(poet-pundits, poet bio-pics, but no poetry),
all a turnoff.

For Ellen this evening there was ocarina emulation,
harps and jazz guitar on the halfpint Yamaha.
Mild interest.

Some space here.

<

/over the fold
(accident on the A6)
it's all manuscripts and mass printlessness,
text art objects, electric sacred-pretend

no, cut that back, make the book

over the fold
for glass boxes, light welling out
kids' glitter all over the audit trail

<

/

look me squarely in the eye

tell me you're not
tell me you're not
tell me you're not
a constructivist

<

/

stapler now, please, we're loose

(a red one lords it in the stuck drawer
of sticker books and weightless costume rings –
'When I grow up I'm going to marry you, Dad.')

<

/

blank inside cover

<

/

We are book makers, bet on it.

Ellen knows 'blurb':
'This book has no front cover.
I am on page 2
with a picture of a dog and Katie.
I am not allowed a dog.
Dad is not being sensible.
I can read music.'

Fold-up

Donny, remember that remainder shop in Soho –
you'd just bought me *Damned to Fame: The Life
of Samuel Beckett*
and I said not two weeks previous
I'd been propositioned
by a woman a few minutes off duty,
for a laugh I guess,
right in front of the Taschen Klimt?

Ian Brown, ex Stone Roses,
rides a fold-up bicycle backwards
right by it in the video
for the single 'Fear'.
It's an acrostic song –
For Everyone a Road, and so on,
not bad going for pop culture,
though it's not always
one word per line (reminds me
of Roy Fisher's abc
in one of Ron King's exquisite pop-ups,
and how 'Auld Lang Syne'
was once the tune
all America learned the alphabet to,
not that that's a nationalist statement,
and then there's Ellen, counting –
how sixes and sevens
are elided if she's not thinking –
it's the sibilant –
'She is only two years old!' –
so she'll go four, five, six, eight,
almost the kind of counting
Tom Robinson sang
just as he was coming out,
a long time before
'presenter material',
and Katie's teacher is saying
she thinks yes maybe Katie
can recognise one to three
(it's eye-pointing, mainly),
and we'll have to watch

the imbalance
between sides of the rib-cage,
first signs of scoliosis already there,
quite possibly, 'classic symptoms',
but Jackie's already
got the facts, met other parents).

When Ian Brown pedals
backwards for miles –
it must be Berwick Street and environs –
all the pedestrians
are in reverse, too,
blurred –

if I can get our recorder to work
I'll tape it and see how it looks
as you rewind it. Of course,
you'll not get the music –
you'll just have to remember
all the instrumentation.

Not your kind of song anyway.

Meet you there on Wednesday morning? Say eleven?

A rising field

You follow dogs –
you want to command them in telepathic Canine
but spoken Human is the training language – 'Good *girl*!', '*No*-oh!', '*Sit!*'

You follow dogs –
sheepdogs, grudgedogs (misunderstood), half-sisters of wolves.
All breeds accepted, no dog too small.

You follow dogs –
sometimes they follow you (friends' dogs, family dogs) –
and now they're pencilled animals, hurtling,
felt-tip assisted, an acceleration of pastels and paint –
you're leading the pack way up the rising field.

You always let me lose.

Little toes

Little toes – too much weight.
A five-year-old's feet
ten years younger / a century older
than the waist-up wrestler,
the armchair dancer
little feet won't support.

All aboard the wheelchair! The whirled chair!
All aboard the world chair! Small world. Small world.

Little toes – almost the right shape –
driftwood / abstract-petite.
'A real work of art' – little big-sister –
my hair-pulling grabster,
my sandwich snatcher,
my thief of too good report.

All aboard the wheelchair! The whirled chair!
All aboard the world chair! Small world. Small world.

All aboard the wheelchair! The whirled chair!
All aboard the world chair! Small world. Small world.

Compartment

When the girls all shook a coke to pass around
I saw my daughter find a lifelong friend
for half an hour – all, surely, Katie's age.

Hopeful look, touch of hand; rare common ground.
'It's your turn – twist the lid, or just pretend!'
(*The pangs of ifs no smile can quite assuage.*)

Katie took the tensioned bomb. She held
then gripped – began to crush the fizzing flask
as if destruction were the game,
as if all belong
   through glee, through wrong,
   indulgent blame.

The girls all cooed a rising No-oh-oh!, repelled
cartoonishly en masse: Katie should bask
in this generosity, become, in their gangish pantomime,
   their celebrity, their beloved dame.

The bottle burst just before they left.
 It speckled brownish paste on every blouse,
   a school crime, I guess. They laughed, all the same.

At the Modern

Ramp-joy –
Katie is an art lover, turbos down
the turbine free Turbine Hall, achieves
avant-garde speed.

The chair is back to metal,
sculptural, velocity-in-mass,
a just-controlled hurtle
hardly in my hands.

<

In the well-labelled lobby
we are clutter.

The able-bodied demand
Rothko, step-free and fast.

They slip round and in,
fill each low-hum lift, tight-lipped.

They are refined, self-sublime.
They stand their ground.

<

Sir Nicholas Serota lacks so much space
in his scant power station.

<

Are we a filmed installation? I
can't quite see.

'Please
keep the Modern
free.'

Mermaid in a wheelchair

Mermaid in a wheelchair,
teenage refugee.

A guest from Atlantis –
a princess, an apprentice –
an island far from me.

Fifty per cent is by continuous assessment

I will be, I will be, I will be
the World's Best Dad.

I said a hundred.
And I want to see your working.

Ninety per cent is by continuous assessment

I will be, I will be, I will be
the World's Best Mum.

I said five hundred,
and I want to see all your working.

Can you tidy up afterwards, love, thanks?
Oh I like what you've tried to do with your hair.

Missing person

I dreamed you played the piano
just like you'd sing 'We're home!'
(The kids steer past you –
polyphony, strophe.)

That was alone, in this future,
advertised – not just a gesture
(a touch, the gesture,
eyes meet, the gesture) –

advertised –

What was the dream
going to say?

The dream can't remember

but 'all', 'chance',
and 'many a December'
play, perfect,
from your calloused fingers.

I took no lessons.

I teach the fugue.

Namesake

I always wanted.
At the age of sixteen I was born,
talented, dynamic, a glamour.

A tough industry to circuit –
few stand.

I'm frank, direct, bold.
(Concern me:
no-nonsense has earned.)

Me, the thinking-man's realistic!
Icon *and* a family,
I suppose.

My future looks looking forward,
sharing my challenging,
my you.

Katrina Amy Alexandria Alexis Infield Price, b. 1978, 'Jordan', England

Namesake

Was artists, actors, dancers,
one of the most.

Timid eyes, expressive darling.
Often received advice.

Royal, legendary, solodanserinde.
Also: the little mermaid.

Heart ballet and acting,
1968.

Ellen Price, 1878-1968, ballerina, Denmark

Faster!

Eeny meeny yak yak,
eeny meeny *Ay!*
Eeny meeny yak yak,
eeny meeny *Ay!*

Ooga booga,
ooga booga.
Ooga booga
slice!

Down-down *day!*
See-see *kay!*

See-see way-a away-a-

eeny meeny yak yak,
eeny meeny *Ay!*
Eeny meeny yak yak,
eeny meeny *Ay!*

Jazz syllabus

The electric piano
just then. The left, the right

apart from everything else.
Harpsichord or Church?

The left and the right,
Harpsichord
or Grand Piano 2.

Strawberry-scented strawberry-coloured
raspberry nail varnish,

a smear on one off-white key.
'Bursting in on me like that.'

High red gates → *prawns, pork*

Eight and your hair up and back
and so twelve perhaps, to a stranger,
a companion today at China China

not knowing completely –
'our annual place' – not knowing completely
just exactly where we are.

Your favourite: 'No music,
and no paintings.'

The paper doors

Two advent calendars –

half a child was saved
with my non-profit
Father Christmas. He has twenty-four
2-D gifts, craved
but 'Not enough for the world!'

What drove Santa holy?

The Nativity competes –
has a chocolate a day
my daughter reports.
Will Christmas be
nougat, or a truffle,
Jesus or a heart?

Wait, one last. The first
my daughters' mother chose
years before the children –
hinged card baubles
fastened to a paper tree.
They opened to candles,
a collared dove. No,

a fourth. You've unlocked
almost every door.
Holly. Mistletoe. One
paper hatch – that… will. not. budge.

Initials

We *can't* go in there.

You didn't know, right?
You... don't – no one's told you, Dad, have they?

No one has told you. I thought you were
'an information professional'.

It does! The founders. No offence – it's just, well,
I'm not. You're not (I know some of your friends –)

I'm not – you know –
I mean I *am* proud.

Playground fact: GAP stands for Gay and Proud

Manmade buoyancy

'Why does *she* have to come?'
Eye-rolling, an adolescent pout.
'She's not family – I'm not
going out.'

'Put your flaming waterwings on.
The sea's never been so fine.
You're both a someone's family:
mine.'

If you fall, or touch a line, your turn ends

At last, the distant beach –
but the sand is grit, the waves lethargic.
Seaweed clogs the shallows.

(Later there'd been a village, a saint's college,
an abandoned 'town', way up beyond the dunes.
Women brought linen down, puritan bundles, black washing
for the shoosh of the sea, its slow flense.

They demanded 'soddening', 'shore trouble', centuries of deadening,
of hard salt cleanse.

All revenge requests were met. It made perfect sense
in 3073
but that was two days home, a get-to-work dream.)

You decided nothing should mean
meanly. We should make the most of the merely seems.
You found softer sand, marked out each line, each number.

Childhood's slumber! – you woke a beautiful creature,
gently, from the dry seabed.
We both watched what you gently did: scratched

a saving ladder,
a net,
a hopscotch grid.

Compartment

Your first fox – 'Black!'

Today, we're telling darkness out
in bright elaboration, 'ash'
or 'charcoal', 'dusk' or 'coalhole', going back
track devout
an age of gazes (rain's light, sun's lash).

Your first fox – 'Black.' Brown
perhaps: 'black' you said, and *I* did, an exact mistake
as if as ifs were actual and colour, never simple, never less than double.
The essence of your first red fox: black, indelible.

I've tried to find more detail about that day, beyond the animal, write it down.
All memory is minimal: it's speech, translating sensation;
        delays, I'm certain, held our train between two stations
        (I think a little of the shorting signals all parents manage to make).

We're single-parent late, at the edge of a briar surge. I can smell the brakes.
        A fox, dark, slight, is master yet of all the rubble.
'Black!' I hear us say, that common urge to share the marvel,

        and I try for more, to forge a detailed fable.
        ('Black!' I hear us say.) I'm just. not. able.

House martins

Back at the old place, I saw two house martins
high up the gable wall.

None had sought to settle there before,
to spit their muddy puddles out and form a property.
They'd preferred our neighbours' roof:
the protection, the liberty, of ample decoration. The darkness there
always was more generous, a home-maker's salvation –
pretty, but hurricane proof.

As darkness thickens, dusk's exhilaration thins.
Now a further martin flitted in.

Steep to good sense, the three gripped the roughcast.
They settled to survey, confer, to attest
(they're squat little scraps at rest):
from a blue-black sketch-of-a-guess
they solidified to a delegation, a thorough inspectorate of doubt.

No soul was about – I called softly, softly.
Less softly, not quite a shout.
At last my daughter clattered out, in pink trademarked clobber.
She slowed, though, at this conspirator,
his mock-sharp glance. She stopped, she stepped – a careful dance
nearer. Beneath our tired travellers
we both looked up – shared
seeing's hush.

A little later she fetched her phone:
no rush – a flourish, but no chatter. I saw her capture
those soft angular shapes, if just as specks (no flash, no zoom).

The eaves were empty when I visited next, early evening / late afternoon.
The martins, I guess, assessed that shelter's future:
took the measure of tomorrow; or at least, made the attempt.
They'd 'talked' at length. They'd paused; paused. Decided against.

SMALL WORLD

Delicate greenery

No colours can mean more than Lego's:
there is strength's ideal in its red, in its blue,
in the boldness of its yellow. Already I see
the ambition of a ski-lift, ascending,
in parallel blocks of bumpy plastic,
up from the patio to the highest ridge
in the low retaining wall.

(In the Eiger rockery there's the soft purple of aubrietia, alyssum's white lace.
The delicate greenery of alpine foliage completes the Suffragette livery –
as if my mother'd arranged a tribute to that vast realisable dream.

I accept the complexity of a childhood apparently organised,
I bear witness even to the gold of wasps –
they are monitoring the fuchsia in its overbrimming bloom.)

I remember, now, three of us, circus-acting my father's stepladders
all the way up our feature stairs.
In a far corner of the breakthroughed loft (otherwise clear)
there were two dark bottles: empty vinho verde.
Each the broad squat trunk of a little tree,
those fat saplings once flourished either side of my parents' field of a bed.
Leafless but protected, each tree would fruit in winter with light,
ample with just one creamy pear.

Later they had been tactilised with Wester Ross shells (a Cub Scout task).
They seemed now shipwreck archaeology,
not bark but encrusted flasks – with the tightest of stoppers.
(A Roman warship had been surprised by barbarian intellect
and all that survived was a conscript's bliss: the promise of fresh water.)

In the half-darkness two boys took Lisa's confession –
Macgregor was her forbidden name, hers a hunted clan.
In return we swore-in our new sister with a few hushed words,
offering, finally, our identities for hers –
our 'sacred animals', our 'spirit beasts',
'Our Creatures of Deepest Soul'.

All were protected by a Red Indian / James Bond curse.
My brother's guardian life-force was a charcoal-soft ghost-horse
(from *Figure 1. Lascaux.*)

Mine had less show – that was my boast.

I'm a mountain fox – not least, not most –
scavenging, thriving, moving between
bin and bone, living always almost alone.

Blue black permanent

after Margaret Tait

A fifties family on the beach
or rather, what the parents watch
nested in their scrubby dunes:
the waddling boys let loose
at the shallows with their sister:
'Higher! Higher! Higher!'

The gentle ocean's weight,
the waves' forgiving height,
the sea's slow
skipping rope:

all
three
jump.

Blue black permanent

That unspooling film
unwraps the windbreak,
the cotton-and-poles
my father'd take
down to a different shore:
he'd unfurl its orange-and-plum
flag-of-no-country
and struggle with the breeze,
the nothing of its catch
flapping in its trawl.
Round the camp of towels
it stuck the shelly grit,
screening, for a time,
a yard or two of calm.

Nimble, oblique

Gran arrives / with a sandy-coloured poodle – / 'Sandy' – /
and six / terracotta pots / asthmatic with geraniums. /
In the hygienic fibre / each little label / is T-shaped, / and off-white plastic /
like a shell – / a shell can't share colour properly. /
In faint blue biro / the word is / 'Gerusalem,' / 'Geronimo', / glimpsed. /
Are you thinking / of a topiary dog? / No – /
his 'mother' / was formal in gardening, /romantic / in animal grooming. /

'Choke-up Chicken,' / she would say / when Sandy coughed. /
Companionship is always / unequal, / in both directions. /
'Three days / and he's still not back,' /
four days and there he is, /dirty haunches / and a panting laugh. /
His tongue / was a rasher with no fat. / He tried BabyBio /
and found it wasn't / essence of rabbit. /I tried BabyBio, /
(a little tongue touch on the hole at the top of its bulb) / – it isn't /
Worcester Sauce. /

'P. is a Pig,' / my father's mother would write, / years before she'd settled /
in the populous colony / of her only child's / distant family. / It was years
ahead /
of the perpetual past, / of recurrent 'would' – / the comfort of pattern./
Perce (Percy (Percival)) – Pa – / was what? / Violent? / Obstinate? / A
little unkind? /
Dad doesn't talk / about anything / but men's marvels: /
he and his father, say, / the last shipwrights / to Kent's fleet of windmills; /
the last cart surgeons, too, / wrapping potatoes / in bandages of broadsheets /
(damp and foreboding) / placing them in makeshift foundries, /
forcing vast wheels / (through flame's harsh tempering) / somehow to mend. /
They were joiners to gentry, / joiners to luck, / to the hundreds' /
speech-oak kings. /

Grandfather has died / and Gran arrives / with a sandy-coloured poodle, /
flaring geraniums / and an appetite / for only the lightest of bread. /
Now there's a woman in a trouser-suit strapped to a trapeze – /
she's oblique, /
hanging diagonally /
from a lantern – /
with grey-and-white stripes / (it's vast, /
moving at speed). /
No, /

she's a 'senior citizen', descending conventionally.
The craft is routine, just a hot air balloon.
But there are flowerpots for ballast round the close-knit basket
and slowly, slowly, she is setting herself down
(she is frail, weightless – real, but lighter). My father
helps her stoop,
                    step,
from solid ship to aerial land.
Sand is unsure, leaps only when his leader is secure.
If 'remember' can be true there's an intensity I cannot anchor:
it's a meeting remaining in its happening,
it was 'so – ' and, so, it is always so.
Finally, though, there's the song that's to become soundtrack for son
remembering mother, a tune Sandy satirises in the break for *The Saint*.
'I can't,' he seems to bark, 'I can't,
I can't let Maggie go.'

Initials

Rich, Pete's added the Newbuild to the round.
Down to the swamp, I don't think. Can't be arsed.
They're yours if you want, a third of my share.
The Senior Price Price Monitor says: market due to grow.
There are scandal readers in them there meshes, kid.

Start at the WIMPEY sign and circle back.
Do you know the acronym concept?
R-I-P for Rest in Peace, I guess.
B-O-A-C,
I-R-A.

No – I tell a lie. A word you can *say*, a word
compressing others.

Posh, Mum says, for Port Out Starboard – .
Starboard – . Whatever the H stands for. WASP
in America: White Anglo Saxon Protestant.
Do you know what the Prods make of WIMPEY?

Playground fact: WIMPEY stands for We Import More Paddies Every Year

38

Pinnacle wordfinder

Kaleidoscope –
competitive interest, memories.

Budding aftershave, railings, fantasising girlfriend –
the corner of the ghost.

I love them, taught to –
'Dream rattling, wake rattling.'
The crows as bad. No,

hop in: the slightly older childhood
in licked glitches, chess piece knuckles.

We drink too much, like a family –
a backlit game, it turns out.

Don't think: absorb.

Prayer

after Apollinaire

When I was little
My mother always dressed me in blue and white
O Holy Virgin
Do you still love me
I know myself
I will love you
Until I die
But it's over all the same even so
I don't believe in heaven or hell
I don't believe anymore I don't believe anymore
The sailor rescued
For always remembering
His daily Hail Mary
Looked like me looked like me

IN MEMORY

Breaking point

in memory

A mother's death leaves a family
a house without a roof.

From a distance all looks sound.
Close up, it's desolation.

A carpenter is used to making structures
for a family, but home-making –
it's not a one-man task.

A mother's death leaves a family

I remember, in the old front room,
loud late nights. We were talking through
the kids, through husband and wife.

No one could mistake
you and I for sister and brother,
wild strawberry blonde, sister.

(We might still be close, talking,
trying to solve your death.)

The children press down on their father –
he takes it, he's a carpenter, he knows breaking point.
Survives.

Fiona, I thought you two were taking me dancing?

Aphasia in last days

in memory

'my hands… together' – let us –
'warm, despite, and knowing –'
let us

'pew is a specific word,
taking a good look at myself'

don't worry everybody
'she had said'
don't worry, everybody
has broken –
about the
you know, broken? –
what do you? broken
('glances, smiles, touches headscarf')
… call it?

'taps her forehead'
the

the brain!

yes
everyone

the brain everyone
has broken down

SMALL WORLD

Relatives Room

In the Relatives Room you don't know.

In the Relatives Room you know
it's OK to use the coffee.
There's milk in the mini fridge.
Don't forget red cap means skimmed,
green semi.

In the Relatives Room you don't know.

In the Relatives Room you know
there are too many flowers.
They're banned from the wards,
'But you can't just bin them, can you?'
(Some lilies are boorish as they go over,
some are lewd.)

In the Relatives Room you don't know.

In the Relatives Room you know
they're an East European family
and you think the father is saying to his wife, to their two sons,
we'll get through this, we'll all get through this,
don't worry.

When the ten o'clock news begins why do they leave?

In the Relatives Room you know
you can't speak a single language,
especially English.

In the Relatives Room you don't know.

In the Relatives Room you don't know.

In the Relatives Room you can't remember
a single number to phone.
You know where your memory is:
it's clammed-up in your mobile, out in Zone 3.
It's back home, paper-weighting six unfinished poems.
One's for Valentine's Day – is it a joke or a poem? You have until next week.

In the Relatives Room you don't know.

In the Relatives Room you know
kindness.
You're not sure if you're hungry but Caroline does
and she brings you toast.
You talk about St Kitt's, Nevis, late shifts. She asks if
you're next of kin –
'We're boyfriend and girlfriend.
"Partners"? Seven years.'
'As good as it gets,' she says.
She touches your shoulder.
There's a paper to sign.

In the Relatives Room you know
the contents in the large grey bag.
You know that bright red purse with the tack-stitch detailing.
You know that black bra, that lime-green sweater.
The knee-length boots were a birthday gift in Provence
(breathless, I held the train for you, neither on nor off).

In the Relatives Room you don't know. You don't know.

In the Relatives Room it is certainly
evening
but it's eight-thirty and it's ten-thirty, now it's early morning,
twenty past two.

In the Relatives Room you know the phone in the handbag
is categorically dead
but Caroline has adapters.
You know there's only one real relative to phone.
You shouldn't phone. What's the point of phoning?
You phone.

Under

A new swimming cap –
a new swimming cap in off-white crêpe.

You're swimming the Atlantic
underwater.

The grumble of the safety boat
is the grumble of the loyal food pump.

Lines –
at full stretch,

spooled out to you,
the hoped-for you, the 'prayed'-for you, the prayed-to you

the 'you', the [you], the you

under.

Lines
asking, asking, asking.

No answer.

The whole ocean

79; 100; 99/52 (68); (6); (15) 19; 5.2

It's you.

You're wired up, tubed up – there's a snorkel too far in.
There's precision engineering; moisturiser.
'If you were a sea creature…'

Mechanical syringes: adrenalin, protein.

On the monitor large soft numbers bubble next to their graph.
They're colour coded. Green's the heartbeat; light blue, breath.
This book of hours is electric, it's a pumped-through aquarium,
it's sampling the darkest zones of the sea.
It's an earnest echo-sounder: muted illuminations pulse –
it's your dynamic ledger of prayer, prayerless, probing higher (deeper)
to faintest life,
beyond all price (priced).

The whole ocean is endangered.

ART is red is blood pressure
and pressure again another soft light blue, the cavity round the heart.
Pressure, pressure, pressure – the tense yellow number
is the brain, its internal push.

You.

You have plastic components and 'Sedation is titrated to body weight' –
morphine's here, as if voluptuous can be synthesised.

Mermaid You, Coral You, the Sea. You're flotsammed, relic'd, unlike.
'If you were a sea creature…'

You're surfaced on a beached life-raft /
you're tangled, subsea,
snagged in a rig, still too deep.

You're the bellows, you're the life support, power all:
the serenity of the machinery, the precision of the staff
(that caring distance is also yours),
your family's on-hold grief.

All strive.
All strive to fathom this aimless curse, this intricate affront.

'Watch the glass, not the sea.'
'Watch the sea, not the glass.'
But the Sea is a secret to itself,
and the Sea would not be capable,
you would not be capable
of remembering your own death,

if you live through it.

Live through it.

Cards

A flower ban across the wards.

Earnest cards.
The people's name for any bloom that thrives at first injury –
for any bloom that thrives paperly –
is *Get-Well-Soon.*

Your bedside gantry is window-boxed with trembling spring.
Green green stems and metal-print petals (all the yellows) twitch.
Precocious February spring!
but, in the air-con gusts,
all flora, all flesh, stays un-refreshed.
This is the longest
inheld breath.

Three days in, blood has been let: soft red, a heart's flower-head
flaunts a single cherished burden. All loves pulse in the sterile garden.

Tradition approves the unsigned Valentine,
and yet
I make myself known:
since you are utterless and utter alone, be in no doubt,
I am your loneliness, your desperate hymn,
your missing person's missing person's glimpse, I am your fugue devout.
You are all within, and I
am without.

Valentine: Would love to meet

Michelin-barred cook, M, 43, seeks undiscrimi-
nating foodlover, F, 47, to share fishy vegetarian
strong-enuff. Has recently impressed with mussels.
Wordsmith, M, 43, WLTM, you know, an F. **Fox**, M, 43,
seeks Hedgehog, F, 47, for rolling around. And
dinner. **Layabout**, M, 43, seeks similar F, 47. No
time-wasters.

All the best

James Tate's sister, 'Yes,
suffered the exact same thing, back in Antigua.

She lived ten years after that.
Not too disfigured. She was much older, of course.

(I hadn't heard. I've been away, visiting my wife's family
back in Vietnam.)

The only thing was... she cried more and she laughed more.
But it's always different – a young thing like your lady!

The allotments aren't an old man's game these days.
You'll die before she will, don't worry.

Yes... she cried more.
She laughed more as well!

You give her James Tate's best wishes.
Tell her: *Tate* sends his *best* wishes.'

Hakan's wife has been in hospital, too.
'(I can't believe it: young couple, double mortgage.
You don't expect it.)

I was. I was fucked. Boys were never taught to cook in Cyprus.
And my "grown-up daughter" *can't fry an egg*.
What can you do?

I had a look at the tyre by the way.
The tyre on your barrow by the way.
It could be the valve. If it's the valve, you're fucked.

Salmon – food poisoning.
The wife's home now, recovering.
She's able to cook so that's a blessing.

All the best, give her all my best.'

54

Corinne

It's Corinne in her grief, they say, singing the sea,
singing the sea.
She lost him, lost her boy. She saw him
lose himself.

Corinne in her grief, they say – singing the sea.

Have I lost my girl? Have I lost her? I never –
I never –

Corinne is grieving. She's grieving. She's
singing the sea, the sea.
She lost her boy. Way out there she lost him.
She saw him – lose himself.

Have I lost her? – my girl. She never –
She never –

The ocean is sullen this morning,
angry – from surface to floor.
You'd know why the silent treatment.
You'd know what all this is for.
(You taught me to swim in the ocean.
You warned me: stay close to the shore.)

Corinne is grieving. She's grieving. She's singing, is she singing
out the sea?

Have I lost her, my best friend? We never –
We never –

We never –

Lift

(You're a first glimpse in a brushed steel lift.
You're black, half-black, part... black. I step towards you.
You wear your hair upswept. Your curls are sculpture, vigorous, 'African'.
You're bantering low. There's a murmur of workmates, a river pool you
                                                    bathe in,
play in, gently trouble.

I can't see them. I'll never know them.
Your eyes are kohled. Your eyes are
grey or blue or green. River eyes, sea eyes.
Kohled – cold?

I'm prose, you're lyric.

There's a ghost of smoke about you – 'giving up again'.
Your scent embroiders the air: delicate little blooms, some fleshly succulents,
mauves, purples, near-blacks; dusk-flowers from a coastal forest –
Botticelli flowers. No, stronger, darker.

(I'm overdubbing trumpets:
Scent to Colour to Music. Musk → Mauve → Music.
Everything is mouths or breathing; inhale, exhale.
And fingers. I have to grasp this gasping glass, this trembling tumbler.
I have to gulp your absent presence down:
delicate, strong, dark. You are beautiful: I sing the word 'beautiful', just to
                                                    myself.

It's wrong to consume. I consume.

Decades of separation (oblivious): almost is near all in its keen nothing.

I've cut myself in the mastering studio. The mixing desk is shorting:
blood is splicing wish with happened, win with lose.
I'm magnifying myself. It's the alcohol.

Viscous and vitreous fuse. Otis was a singer. Otis is a lift.
I'm not brittle in the drunkard lens, I am your equal.
(I am almost your equal.)

We're in tropical woodland. Not a metaforest: we're accidental, we're eventual
                                                    but we're actual.

We're sipping the seconds of 'flower-kissers', hummingbirds:
we're glimmer, we're hover, we're veer.

(I'm a human shape in a brushed steel lift. I'm a distortion behind you,
a smudge on a semi-reflective wall.

You step past, away, out. The doors close, slowly enough.)

(I'm a human shape in a brushed steel lift. I'm a distortion behind you,
a smudge on a semi-reflective wall.

You step past,
away,
out.

The doors close,
slowly enough.)

As if the equal

after Sappho

It's as if the equal – more than the equal – of a god is facing you,
sitting with you (she's listening close) –
and you're speaking sweetly

oh and her beautiful laugh –

now the heart in my chest is fluttering, I'm winging this,
and then I look, just for a second,
and that's my voice gone –

as if –

no, the tongue is broken, there are just licks
of fire under my skin,
my eyes are blind, drumming and only drumming
fills my ears.

A chill of sweat is gripping, shaking me,
I'm as pale as grass.
I am dead. It's as if
I am dead.

But all must be risked.

Frank O'Hara was a curator

for BK

Hey, I'm a curator! I'm a poet!
Today it's elephant dung sublime –
Chris Ofili and his temple of the monkey.
I'll put the colours in here
once we've seen it.

OK, no complications –
this is almost all you can ask
of a two-hour lunch hour.
Facetious has all the vowels
to soften the facts. Irreverence R Us.

Co-workers of the World Unite!
(but only in pairs & Prêt à Manger –
that's French isn't it? –
and without Diet Coke
let's keep things light –
it doesn't mean you're not
the Bee's Knees.
Not only initially,
you are the Bee's Knees.)

*Ah, that's the buzz over – swipe, click,
14.30. 'Back to work happy, very
possibly so.'*

From Crete

Thyme honey. Dancing
on the backs of bulls.

A bee, a friend.

Dominion claim

Shyness – yet,
            finger touched to lips.
                        Led.

Royal procession –
tribute, a possession.
Dragged gentle, torture-teased (king-sized bed).

Fingertips, eye-flickers. Nothing said.

Vocal breathing, pre-speaking,
surge, intimate crowd.

All acres
aching, allowed.

Riot.
Lust's loot.

High rebels, a revel, a ravelling low.

Loyal libertines. Rabble of two.

'A second's scalding'

after Vallejo

A second's scalding
across the sum total of desire's little flesh,
piquant vagrant chilli pepper
at two in the immoral afternoon.

Glove of hems hem to hem.
Fragrant touched truth alive, connecting
lubricious antenna
with an estimate of our being minus knowing.

Maximum ablution washing dregs.
Travellers' cauldrons
that clang and splash with fresh shadow,
unanimous, the colour, the fraction, the hard life,
    the eternal hard life.
Don't worry. That's death.

A lover's blood crying out
deliciously, taking so much
to such a ridiculous point.
And the circuit
between our poor day and the vast night,
at two in the immoral afternoon.

'In the corner there'

after Vallejo

In the corner there, where we slept together
so many nights, I've at last
sat down (still travelling). The sofa for defunct lovers,
has been removed – or who knows just what's come to pass.

You're not here now. It's the corner where,
remember, we were reading that night? Side-by-side?
Your gentle advice! I always did say I loved your tips! Remember
the secret poems, my Apollinaire? It's the corner
I will always love best – don't doubt it.

I'm determined to remember days
of lost summer, your coming and going,
too little and too much, pale, room to room.

On this rainy night,
both far off, I jump suddenly.
It's two doors, opening and shutting,
two doors the wind is opening, shutting
shadow   to   shadow.

Stella

Once, when you were 'travelling',
I forced an early night on solitude.

Still before tomorrow
(though all Tottenham seemed still)
I found myself awake again.
Upstairs, the rising sound roused me –

the slow, jabbed sobs of Stella, making love.

cell

after Virna Teixeira

no morphine can sedate this hurt
passing through the narrow corridor, reaching a room,
opaque glass in the door, a hermetic chamber
and hands, twisted, in the marble

fortification of blood-red souvenirs, acrylics
a flight of fire stairs useless for smoking

needles and lines to embroider repairs

Storming

Epilepsy, perhaps.
Temperature
                    beyond the hollow roof.
The last lapse –
if the last – and loss whole. Hope – hope
                    beyond control. Hope
          reshaped – denied. Shy
          hope. Hope
          fact-aloof. Hope's rise, hope's slide,
          hope's
          harsh reproof.

' "Storming", for want.'
'Not uncommon.' 'Not yet known.'
'A cosmic mystery – if I'm precise.
          A cosmic mystery – if I'm blunt.'
'All life fights, at the last, alone.'

A fit – electricity, at least.
Temperature
                    aspiring (to the fevered sun).
Future held / dropped. The watch
                              increased.
One, one, one.

Fight! Fight with head lightning for peace.
Fight storm with storm, harm
          with electro-cauterising harm.
          Let life's stop cease.

Talks about talks

The Family Room is not the same as the Relatives Room

At some point, relatively soon, we'll have to have a talk.
I mean, did you ever discuss it? Do you know what she would want?

Boyfriend shakes his head. Sister shakes her head. Mother
shakes her head.

Well, this isn't the time to talk about it.
There is still time but we're here because there isn't a lot of time.

I don't want to alarm you but I want to be straight with you.
It's a quality of life issue and I'd like you all to think about it.

Boyfriend. Sister. Mother.

You do know this could be as good as it gets?
Did you never discuss it?

Boyfriend, sister, mother.

If you fall, or touch a line, your turn ends

No teams, and I remember I lost – all stagger and self-protecting clown.
It was close between second and whoever won, but the winner has gone.

We were daft-laughing, obliterating the grid and its numbers,
returning order, back with a skidge.

Afterwards, I sat on a fragment of 10.
I'd be fine alone, watching you both, down at the edge.

(You're beyond the hindered surf:
you're together, splashing spray at each other – spiteless contention –
there's affection, glancing between you.

You're edging out, in deliberate step,
you're finding the right depth. You're saying (I can guess), 'Careful, mind,'
as you make your dive. You're never friends
but can share the waves, defy the land,
swimming together in the clear free Sound.)

That passing place

An orchid, dainty,
petals just pink, embroidered,
brave at the roadside.

Glasgow Coma Scale

first week

Patient: *The Patient.*
Eyes: *Closed.*

('God', eyes closed, makes no sounds, makes no movements.)

second week

Patient: *The Patient.*
Eyes: *Closed.*

('God', eyes closed, makes no sounds, makes no movements.)

third week

Patient: *The Patient.*
Eyes: *Open.*

(eyes closed, no sounds, no movement)

She wakes in war poetry

She wakes in war poetry, ache, slow aware.
'Shrapnelled then.'

She wakes in famine footage, woozy as a foal. A dapper fly
rests on her cheek: he's whispering church latin.

A murmur of practised concern, a wingbeat, a word.
The fly – prune black, clot light –
is whispering, licking sweat, gargling her, swilling, swallowing.
His sorry is slurry – he's sicking her juices
right back up, thickened.
He's re-sipping the soup, pope's broth.
He's lap lap lapping gut gazpacho, girl gruel.

In the women's ward, first dibs.
It's his belief the immobilised meek are his: he inherits them. It's a
                                                    paralysis picnic
with his privilege to probe: no challenge, no question, a lesson.

Boys do savour better – he's pricked many a pucker. Lads keep mum
or police and papacy provide protection: moans will be muffled.
The females, too, are no real trouble and Cardinal Vespa pledges
one more tour of cute intensive care secures the Bishopric of Galway.

She wakes in war poetry.
There's machinery in her lungs. There has been buzzing, maybe.

Someone… who *is* her someone – *he* is? *he* is?
Someone who is *her* someone – *she is his* –
scatters a scar, scatters a, not scatters, not a scar,
scares, scares a dapper fly.

Her someone and she
shoo a priest.

Rose

'Peace!'
'Peace!' Rose is shouting.

No, it's 'Teeth!'
'Teeth! Teeth! Teeth!'

'Teeth,' she says, quietly.
'I just want my teeth.'

Drugs or

At night, small creatures gain the building.
They forage, they leap prettily like squirrels
but they have no tails.

Larger than mice, they hide beneath
the mobile cabinets. They bide, concealed
by all-direction wheels.

(They must be coming up on the lifts –
or the windows need mesh.)

Men made of shadows also slip in.
They just stand there, at the foot of the bed,
then they move on.

Tilt table

Sometimes he sleeps standing up –
he gathers the billows of the polymer curtain around him –

or he's lucky and the little bunk, I think it's up near the nurse's station,
is free.

Most nights, though, he folds himself up like an extra blanket
and rests among the day splints, just beyond my feet.

He's been known to *roll* himself up –
like John Anderson my jo.

I have liked but I have never loved Chagall.
There is something too simple about angels.

He feels the cold even here.
The thick blankets they use are for long service.

At times the tilt table in the special gym is all that's available.
He's found a way to stop it swivelling? but he can't prefer it.

I know this can't be true, or I've come to compensatory new senses.
This all belongs to dream, premonition, déjà vu –

but I am extravagantly awake,
I am open to all messages.

('Angel' only means 'messenger'.)

Last night, after he thought I was asleep,
he settled down in a basket lined with prescriptions.
He was soon snoring like a food pump.

A little later I saw him, eyes still closed, sitting up,
clutching at a slip.
He cried out, 'Another prize-winning poem!',
as if mocking a disgrace.

No one on the ward wakened.

'At least I'm a doctor,' he mumbled, quietening again, whispering his own consolation:

'The pharmacists will understand.'

Clip

The ventilator has been replaced: I can see your face properly.

I stayed up last night, watched a tiny video I'd made just last year.
You're in the open-air pool behind our guest-house in San José,
São João I mean, of course, way up in Minas Geraís.
It was a cold dark room but there were fresh cakes for breakfast!

Explain me your word 'poet'.

Your hair is held with a clip and not a lock is wet.
When you swim close you look up. You ask:
'What's the matter, is the camera broken?'
You swim away but turn your head to call out,
'Are you coming in?'

The ventilator has been replaced: I can see your face properly.

You are breathing, almost solo
(you're still on life support – 'lite')
and now you've opened
both your eyes:
strongly, fully, blue.

(Only translations remain
of what we were. We were pre-translation. Your film doesn't run
in every application.)

Explain me your word 'poet'.

'What's the matter? Is the camera broken?'

Jewellery ☹

The first time the Patient is offered antidepressants, it's a Friday night.
A nurse has been slapping her.

The problem is this: the Patient hates the NG feed.
That's the tube that's pushed up her nose
and then down the back of her throat
and finally into her stomach. NG: 'NasoGastric'.

She has to have it, the nurse tuts at her.
When the Patient turns away she gives her a slap,
hard, brings her face back.
Do you want to starve? You're a spoilt child.

The tube at last is in place. That wasn't so bad was it?
The Patient, a defiant Suffragette, snatches it out.

Eyes meet.

Another slap.

<

The nurse in question wears a nun's headscarf.
She has a necklace with a delicate little gold cross.
The Patient is wearing headgear, as well,
(bandages) and jewellery –
she has a plastic bracelet which bears her date of birth
and a misspelt version of her name.
She has a pendant, too: it's the tracheostomy,
punched into her throat to help her breathe.

As she can't speak the Patient points: she's been allowed six symbols.
They're on a wipeable laminated card.
'I am sad,' the very circular face can be taken to say.
It has a perfect upside-down smile.

<

On his Monday morning rounds the doctor sees the Patient.
She points to the little face.
He turns to his students to share his experience:
'Neurological injury often leads to clinical depression,' he says.

He talks softly to the Patient: 'I know just the pills for this.'

Phantom limb

The Patient didn't lose any limbs: others have just stumps.

The woman in the next bed has a high, sweet, sickly smell
which is gangrene. (Gangrene has a high, sweet, sickly smell:
it stays with you, or its idea does – it's the refrain
    in an angry melodic song).

Beatrice seems simple, she eats only jam sandwiches, makes sure
                                        she can smoke.
She blocks the unit's fire exit with her wheelchair and lights up.
She refuses to wear her artificial leg. It sits upright on a visitor's chair,
                                          as if uncouth.

Sometimes the Patient senses her own 'phantom limb'.
It itches a few inches from her real arm, which she can't sense at all.

Left neglect

lect	neglect
trauma	suffered trauma
brain	half of the brain
reduced	radically reduced
left	objects on their left
'blind'	the 'blind'
'seen'	be 'seen';
finished	regarded as finished
untouched	half remains untouched.
patient	any text the patient
left	the page's left.

> **FactBox: Left neglect**
>
> Patients who have suffered trauma
> in the right half of the brain
> can experience radically reduced
> perception of objects on their left.
> Visitors approaching on the 'blind'
> side of the patient will not be 'seen';
> a meal is regarded as finished
> yet a stark half remains untouched.
> When reading any text the patient
> ignores all words on the page's left.

It's work to sit still

It's work to sit still, busy oblivion.
Meet the deadline but tend to her classical guitar,
hope highly to be tended.

Idle is someone else, picturing handsome.
The warmth in flesh is superfast, but just for loopback's else.
There's self-to-self via golden pelt, cerebral-lubricious.
Low temperatures live on the lonely,
flaunt cold photons (pixels, print) of scripted happy, heat.
This skin, adapted to the light, is the eye, me, a bag in a bag, boiling.
I see your double, turning,

but 'Walk, she can walk.' She – you – you're not up
to stumble, can't muster lust-for-life. I choke back all our lasts –
a viscous sniff since thirst's so thick with grief.
Implicit certainty, secure in its titled past,
has sentenced 'live and love' to just belief. I open a peek
of unjust everything (lust, pre-kiss, is overprimed, beyond mere most).
                                        I am learning Slow
fast. 'Just, just, just.'

Tutor me, electric lutherer. We'll ditch the classics – I have spark bridge,
pickups deluxe.
I need re-build, know-how, the can-do flourish. No,
sequence this static reverb; sequence, sequence, sequence;
spoil me with suite treatment, electronica, meddlement –
                                        I have euphoria to orchestruct.

Spin me off in bundling – I'm as thin as film,
film of the film of our innocent final tour.
(We're tourists not travellers, I always insist it, direct to shot.)
Miss / Mrs / Ms, please, post-produce me, mess with. I can't quite trust
just the resale cult of director's cut. Since you don't ask, I'll be a broken part
of populous before I pledge Pure's private silence, Holy's hold-back hoax. I am
no perfect archive of a person, too good for air, light
(I can't think the task isn't right
to risk a public, its slight, its astound.)

Amp is to yearn is to the size of a house.
There's a glint of love in secure metallurgy, and lock and key:

a gold rush needs its back-home railings, its vault; thirsts a single red
guitar. (Gold
equals red, sunshine, cold control of lush.)

*Each year the open forest diminishes — by three pangs and a brutal equivalence,
and we did so walk in gentle dapple my rambler.*

São Paulo is no city for walkers

'You're still beautiful, all things considered,' – a visitor
pats your wheelchair handle, or we're a slowing eddy, fast
turning back from a sudden slip-road. São Paulo stop. Stop
memorising us as holiday fit, the big Back Then,
casually Casualty-free. Colloquial heart attacks –
the joke's on the joke, so humour me. Ditch that nifty trick
(time travel). It lands us wrong, back. It's all one step two step
and a tragedy under there. ('Remember' kills us stone
beautiful.) Mantelpiece us, for later's trust. I'm happy
with sealable sorrow, tactless visitors we'll still love.

Dust in the tread

A walking boot – Brazilian dust still in the tread –
protects the senseless foot. You're an enemy, Door Jamb.

'Threshold me! – Try lifting *this* boxy rig, loverboy!'
(Tubular steel / Mind the wheels, romance's inscription in health.)

No one has died. No grief allowed.
Grievous harm is the merest term –
decades of life decay, day and day.

'Get over yourself!', beneath all clambering beauty.
Absolutes, superlatives, bomb-plumes of exclamation
tell my reduction. I'm histrionic, max vol, shoutish thinking aloud.

Lovely-couples-walking-lovingly-in-love, walk past,
walk on by for bliss. No offence. No delusion – of you.
I am not alone, and love is not luv and if this
is bitterness it has no direction, or never yours –
I'm all ifs and buts, justified unjust. I crave self-applause
and my anger mopes:
hand-in-hand's trekking hyphenation

                                       dashes hopes.
We cannot love back to forest path, secret shore,
to dune, to view from Version 1
(from Paraty, from São João del Rei, Ben An).

We are compelled to be humbled,
laid low before stroll, amble.

There never was a photo of the happy couple –
imagined self-containment takes 1-2-1 snaps.

Introductions

Anthony is one of the few who can walk.

He knows who he was –
a guitarist and a song writer.
And a do-it-yourself lutherer –
thirty years ago he hammered up
his first instrument, an electric,
from plyboard and wire.
'Devised my own pick-ups,
back then.'

There were no Top Tens, but success enough –
to be alone.

Every day he says Hello
politely, circumspectly; searching.
'I'm Anthony,' he adds,
as if we've only met.
In fact, we've spoken
each and every day
for half a year.

(I introduce myself. I act…
a first encounter.)

Sometimes he seems to know
his feelings are at stake,
but which feelings?
He'll say, 'Of course,
of course you are,'
but there's no memory there.

I don't believe. I don't believe there is
any memory there.

We talk – the Patient, Anthony and I –
until lights out. A nurse calls time.

'I was only admitted yesterday,' he says to me.
'I wonder – would you mind? – guiding me? –
back to my bay?'

Locked

Your wheelchairs locked when I brought Katie up –
I'd misjudged proximity. She
> smiled at the scrape, and *you* smiled, gently.

(Days when you'd laugh, days when you two would play.
> Days when – .)

You are
mermaids on the mend. (It's just a belief.)

You've had three wheelchairs since then,
each less 'hospital', each more 'street' –
yours and Katie's meet
in council teenage cool.

I'll drop the Atlantis romantics, make that the rule.

Katie still toddles, the urban village village fool –
'Lurch' to girls who,
> with different chromosomal luck,
would have been her bestest friends.

You've yet to return to work.
Katie leaves school when the next term ends.

Two Ians and a witch

An Ian at the water's edge straps the woman to the device, a stool on a
sturdy boom.
He pivots her out. She's above the hunger, locked –
an inch about the licks.

An Ian in the water – the famished blue is shoulder high – calls up.
'Ready?' (He is ready, she is ready – is Dry Ian ready?)

All three count.

Into the licks.

If you sink you're innocent, if you swim you're a witch.
If you sink you're innocent, if you swim you're a witch.
('Sink: clean as death.' 'Swim: damned to breath.')

She…
swims.

An award-winning documentary

The BBC are making a documentary today.
The crew crowds the art room but some patients can still be accommodated.

Look, there's a problem, the producer is saying. We have a problem.
                                                                    Anonymity
won't work after all. It just won't.

We're trying to make a powerful story here, a sensitive one.

You are lovely people.
It's all about justice, and you.

I do know what I'm doing! I did go to Cambridge!

<

Look, would you sign a new form? Would you do that for us?

We need to make it more natural, see the whole you,
have you speaking. You speak so beautifully – did you realise that?

I know we said 'just hands', but realistically…

Just to clear that, with the legal guys.

<

I'm afraid there really isn't time for you to think it over.
I wish there was.

<

The thing is, if you don't sign the whole day will be ruined.
No one wants that. No one could possibly want that.
Have you any idea how much a film crew costs?

<

I've been told you've been making a picture of a beach,
Collage can be surprisingly creative, can't it?
Cornwall, was it? I hear you both love Cornwall.
With your partner's daughter, too?

I think people would like to see how well you're coping,
hear how art is working for you.
The other patients – well. They can't exactly be chatterboxes can they!
You are lucky, in your own way.

<

Think of the hospital.
Hospitals need champions these days.

<

We think it could be an award-winning documentary, actually.
Life-affirming. Insightful. And show the real good of the unit.

Not the Film Unit! The unit here, the Stroke Unit.

<

<

Good.

(Gerry – she's signed.)

It's the first day of summer dresses – you're in turquoise hospital slacks,
an old grey T-shirt with slashed neck, loose All Stars (red-wine red).

('Let's just slip these on, shall we?')

I can just judge the precise angle.
You can just reach, touch, the splintered picnic table,
footplate permitting. Just, just, just.

You're yourself, but not left-handed.
With your learning right you're lusting back a viscous juice,
trembling, rippling the fluid.

'Delicious. So much oranger, you know, than speech-therapy liquid.
That swallow test! – and now, to drink like this, to quench this drought
on a humid afternoon, on this day pass lease,' (you're running out of
breath, breathe).

'Even just to watch your lips, your gulp! – You best bitter lush!'

'Cheers!' I say, and you say, 'Cheers, right enough!' Cheers. CHEERS.
(Cheers).

The Elderfield

On our second visit the 'Everfield' is the Elderfield.
We agree we're telepathic. We're fond of 'Ever'.

At an open air trestle, we're at last alone.
We have half an hour.

'I,' we say together, and 'No! – you first.'

In the pause a large man appears.
He lights a cigarette.

'I'm a Russian Lithuanian,' he insists, as if we'd asked.
He touches my shoulder.

'I admire you. I want to buy you a drink.
Is it Stella? It's fine if it isn't Stella. You can have Stella.'

He glances at you, then looks back to me.
He tries to make me meet his look.

'Most husbands wouldn't do this,' he says,
tapping my shoulder with a flick of the back of his hand. 'Take them out.

Did she have your children?

I'm a father. I have a little baby, five weeks old,
but the lady in question... I'm very well paid.'

<

It's twenty minutes later:
you are still playing vegetative state.

I am improvising interruptions:
'We're just here for some precious time together,'

'We're just here between hospital sessions,'
'We're just here –'

Four black-hatted men walk briskly past.
Their long side-ringlets have their own rhythm.

(Is the hair soft or is it like wire?)

The 'Russian Lithuanian', who is 'a father and very well paid',
touches my shoulder for the fifth or sixth time.

'Shalom!' he calls to the men.
'Shalom!' they return, briefly facing us. They don't stop.

Our 'friend' leans into us, forces smoke out through his nose.
'Would she like another juice?' he asks.

'Can your wife understand anything?'

Gallery

Suspended from a wire are seven panes of the thinnest glass.
The glass is so light there seems no tension in the line:
all stress is interior alone.

Each has been etched with the cross-section of a tree,
　　　about forty close-set rings.
The panes are immaculate. Only the etched circles are visible –
the hard surface bearing them cannot be seen.

The rings are so thin they could be thread.
Though born from acid, from force, they could be drawn by hand,
slowly, by a gifted child.

On each pane there is a golden ravelling,
gentle, a loose knot of golden braid.

Year after year the Patient will have seen this:
I have forgotten to wind that line in before!

Autumn always brings this light to her garden, and to its patient bright spiders.

I am greatly changed

Great Expectations

That poor dream, as I once used to call it,
has all gone by. (The freshness of beauty
is the saddened softened light
of once proud eyes.) I have very often – .

I intended to come back. Tracing, proving.
I thought – . I thought you would like – .
'God bless you, God forgive you!'
you said to me.

I am greatly changed.
I thought you would like to shake hands.
What I had never felt before
was the friendly touch.

I very often hoped – .
I have often
thought of you.
An imaginary case.

I have been considerate and good,
I have been bent and broken,
suffering, God forgive you.
Suffering, God bless you.

(Suffering has been stronger
than all other teaching,
a heart to understand
what my heart used to be.)

The ground belongs!
Everything else,
little by little, has gone.
I wonder you know me.

If you could say to me then
'God bless you! God forgive you!'
you will not hesitate now.
('God bless you,' you said to me.)

Poor, poor old place!
Ruined place.
Would I step back?
Ignorant, held?

She gave me her assurance
(her voice, her touch).
I took her hand,
evening mists rising now, tranquil.

'We are friends.'

Release & the goodwill aquifers

No, we'll not accept Hospital Transport.
A week ago, you're alone in our old front room, a trial run –
I'm at work for this 'real life situation' – you're weak, can't walk an inch.
Four hours late, a self-important fluorescence, a haste-fraud, an emergency
nonchalance, finally turns up.

'Out-sourced ambulance'.

I meet that private sector excellence, that efficiency gain, back at the ward:
'Why didn't you just tie her to a radiator, slap her about a bit,
text me a rendezvous for the ransom?'

He looks hurt, and I am – I shouldn't have said 'her'. He
doesn't answer.

Now that his super-light stretcher is empty, he tucks the straps back, steers
wearily out.

No, we'll not accept Hospital Transport.
A last juice, a last London Pride and then we'll take the two-bus option,
compete
with sleeping babies in padded buggies, their mother guards.

We raise a glass in advance: Here's to the big red crates!
And praise for Kenya and Ghana, Nevis & St Kitts.
Nigeria, Poland, Botswana – praise for all the nurses!
Almost all the nurses. Thank you, thank you, thank you.
The Philippines! – thank you nurse, thank you doctor!
(We are a people-thief nation: forgive this kingdom of traffickers.
And here's to cause's cure.)

No, we'll not accept Hospital Transport,
but now I'm a mellow Prider. Praise for that driver.
I know, I know, I do know: I've been all misdirected anger,
blame game adrenalin, 'above criticism'. 'We've had enough of collapse, of
paroxysm.'

Elderfield, Everfield, let the me seep back in, let us all seep back
to the best of ourselves, fill the lack, restore the wells.

We sup up, wheel out.

(At our front door I fumble for my keys. You hand me yours.)

AFTERWORD

Fliers

Professor Konte asks if I feel failed by friends,
by partners, relatives I once trusted.
Never.

I should detail my thanks,
mount a counter mail-shot: they deserve tributes.
Friends and family aren't just a tariff,
they don't need Mr Konte's insinuations.

Professor Konte is black-and-white magic and black-and-white litho'd:
sometimes he's a simple chit among other flier litter
(pizza delivery, and plumbing offers I may well need to take up).
Sometimes he's a business card, slicker than my own.

I keep his details, but only in a folder for 'possible art projects'.
(I've become obsessed with Christianity and voodoo,
their lantern shapes, their motto menace.)
I keep them far from the taxi cards, from roofers' numbers,
and far, too, from my Bible. It was my mother's:
absurd; beautiful; hers.

The years.

I have been lonely but I have done nothing alone –
I'm not sure they know, more than once, more than twice, family have saved my
                                                        life. Yes,
family – and friends – have walked me back from the ledge –
it was all done by text, by pints, by tactical gifts.
'It was nothing, just what anyone would do', 'Meet you in the Plough',
'I hope you don't mind, I'm cooking tonight: three courses fine?'
I should detail my thanks but they're firmly against
micro-immortalisation –
we're too close for that, they caution,
you'd be drying the cat... in a microwave oven.)

Only the Patient offers consent – to leave, we both believe, 'the Patient' bound
                                                        in this book
and my lover freed.